Colossians & Philemon

Christ In You

"The Hope of Glory"

Dr. Billy J. Owensby

©2021

CHRIST IN YOU
THE HOPE OF GLORY
Copyright © 2021 by Dr. Billy J. Owensby

All rights reserved. No part of this publication may be reproduced, distributed, or transmitted in any form or by any means, including photocopying, recording, or other electronic or mechanical methods, without the prior written permission of the publisher or author, except in the case of brief quotations embodied in critical reviews and certain other noncommercial uses permitted by copyright law.

Although every precaution has been taken to verify the accuracy of the information contained herein, the author and publisher assume no responsibility for any errors or omissions. No liability is assumed for damages that may result from the use of information contained within.

Library of Congress Control Number: 2021910066
ISBN-13:   Paperback: 978-1-64749-473-5

Printed in the United States of America

GoToPublish LLC
1-888-337-1724
www.gotopublish.com
info@gotopublish.com

Contents

Title	Page
(Introduction)	v
Colossians 1:1-8	
Colossians 1:9-12	
Paul's Prayer For The Saints	5
Colossians 1:13-23	
The Preeminent Christ	7
Colossians 1:24-29	
Paul And The Hidden Mystery	15
Colossians 2:1-7	
Built Up In Christ	19
Colossians 2:8-15	
Made Complete In Christ	23
Colossians 2:16-23	
Have You Been Robbed?	31
Colossians 3:1-11	
Focus, Forsake, And Follow	33
Colossians 3:12-17	
The Christian's Wardrobe	39
Precepts of Life	43
Colossians 3:17-25	
Colossians 3:18-4:1	
Family And Work Relationships	45
Colossians 4:2-6	
Devoted Prayer And Godly Conduct	53
Colossians 4:7-18	
Paul's Co-Laborers In The Ministry	57
Philemon	63
Works Cited	69
G.O.S.P.E.L.	71
About The Author	73

Colossians
Christ In The Universe
(Introduction)

Colossians is one of the shortest of Paul's letters, but it is perhaps one of the most exciting. The letter is addressed to the church at Colossae. It is not definite that Paul ever visited Colossae. However, the thought of many is that Paul possibly visited Colossae while on his third missionary journey.

The Colossian Epistle was written by Paul while he was a prisoner in Rome in A.D. 62. According to Colossians 4:7-8, Tychicus delivered the letter. The purpose and occasion regarding the writing of this Epistle was that Paul was sending a messenger to Philemon who was in Colossae, concerning Onesimus, a runaway slave who had been converted (4:7-9). Also, Epaphras had brought Paul news of the church in Colossae which included several encouraging things but also disturbing news of false teaching that was leading some away from the truth of Christ.

Colossians is referred to as the sister Epistle of Ephesians. The central theme of Colossians is Christ while the theme of Ephesians is the church. Also, some have noted the theme of Colossians as Christ In the Universe and the theme of Ephesians as The Cosmic Significance of the Church. The Colossian Epistle contains seventy-five verses that are also found in the Epistle of Ephesians. Paul does not confront the heresies point by point but he shares truth in a positive manner. The subjects that the apostle touches on are:

1. Inordinate attention being given to the powers of the spirit world.

2. The undue attention that was given to the observances of feats, fasts, new moons, and Sabbaths (2:16), and circumcision (2:11).

3. The influence of Gnosticism, a heresy that plagued the church in its first 200 years of existence.
- ✓ Gnosticism is derived from the Greek word gnōsis, meaning knowledge.
- ✓ Gnostics separated matter from thought.
- ✓ Gnostics believed that the body of Christ was something that appeared to be material, but really was not.
- ✓ Gnostics believed the spirit was entirely separate from the body. For that reason, they were not re- sponsible for the acts of the body. This led to an immoral lifestyle.
- ✓ In Colossians 2:9 Paul stressed plainly and clearly that in Jesus Christ dwelt all the fullness of the Godhead bodily. He truly was God in the flesh. Paul stresses that spirituality is not achieved by severe self-discipline and avoidance of all forms of indulgences for religious reasons (asceticism), but putting on Christ and setting one's affections on Him. Also, he stresses that one is to strip away or put off all things that are contrary to Christ's will (2:20-3:11). Paul had no problem with Jews keeping religious practices. However, this was not to be done as a reason for obtaining salvation. Jew and Gentile are saved in the same way, by faith in Christ alone.

Finally, is should be understood that true wisdom is the mystery of God in Christ, who indwells all of those who receive Him as Savior and Lord.

Colossians 1:1-8

1:1 "Paul an apostle (apŏstŏlŏs) of Jesus Christ by the will of God, and Timothy our brother."

Apostle: (apŏstŏlŏs) Paul is a "sent one." He is a delegate and ambassador of the Gospel. Officially Paul is a commissioner of Christ. He has been sent according to and by "the will of God." Timothy is a constant companion of Paul. According to Acts 16:1, Timothy was from Lystra. Paul takes him with him while on his second missionary journey.

1:2 "To the saints and faithful brethren in Christ who are at Colossae; Grace to you and peace from God our Father."

The "saints" are considered to be holy ones, those who have been set apart. These saints are referred to as "faithful" (pistŏs), which is to say they are sure, true, and trustworthy. They were faithful in their conduct and belief. The term brethren refers to a special relationship they have with Christ. The apostle greets and extends to them grace (the free gift of God), and peace (the full blessings of life) which comes from the Father.

James 1:17 "Every good thing given and every perfect gift is from above, coming down from the Father of lights, with whom there is no variation or shifting shadow."

1:3 "We give thanks to God, the Father of our Lord Jesus Christ, praying always for you."

"Thanks to God" (euchristĕō) is to express ones gratitude and to be grateful. Paul is giving thanks to God for the people. The apostle was praying always, there was a regularity in his prayers.

1:4 "Since we heard of your faith (pistis) in Christ Jesus and the love (agapē) which you have for all the saints."

Paul had heard of their faith (pistis) which was in Jesus Christ. The term faith is evidence of their conviction, persuasion, and credence regarding religious truth. The (agapē) love can be defined as benevolence, affection, and also charity.

1:5 "Because of the hope (ēlpis) laid up for you in heaven, of which you previously heard in the word of truth, the gospel (ĕuaggĕliŏn)."

The hope (ēlpis) spoken of by the apostle is one of anticipation, expectation, that is with confidence. It is a hope that is laid up or reserved in heaven. They had previously heard and had this hope because of the gospel (ĕuaggĕliŏn), the good message from the Word of truth, which is opposed to that which is false.

1:6 "Which has come to you, just as in all the world also it is constantly bearing fruit and increasing even as it has been doing in you also since the day you heard of it and understood the grace of God in truth."

The truth has gone into all the world and was spreading abroad, always guaranteed to bring forth fruit. The saints of God had heard and come to know or understood (ĕpiginōskō), which is to say they had become fully acquainted with and acknowledged the truth of the Gospel.

1:7 "Just as you learned it from Epaphras, our beloved fellow bond-servant, who is a faithful servant of Christ on our behalf."

Epaphras is given his first introduction in the Epistle of Colossians. He is characterized by Paul as one who is beloved, a faithful <u>servant</u> (sundŏulōs), which is to say a co-slave, and a minister of the same master. Also, he is said to be a fellow bond <u>servant</u> (diakŏnŏs), a waiter of tables, an attendant, one who runs errands, a deacon, and a minister.

1:8 "And he also informed us of your love in the Spirit."

Epaphras informed Paul of their love (agapē). This is a divine love that does not count the cost, it gives sacrificially. It was all done in the Spirit (pnĕuma).

Colossians 1:9-12
Paul's Prayer For The Saints

1:9 "For this reason also, since the day we heard of it, we have not ceased to pray for you and to ask that you may be filled with the knowledge of His will in all spiritual wisdom and understanding."

Paul's prayer was one of earnest. The word "pray" is (prŏsĕuchŏmai) which is to pray to God, to supplicate, to pray earnestly for. Paul prays for the saints to be filled with knowledge (epignōsis), which is to have a full appropriated knowledge of the truth with recognition and discernment. This discernment was regarding God's will (thĕlēma) which is His purpose, desire, and decree. Paul's prayer includes requests for wisdom (sŏphīa) in the spiritual (pnĕumatikŏs) sense which is divine and not carnal, and understanding (sunĕsis) which is to mentally put together, referring to intellect and knowledge.

1:10 "So that you will walk in a manner worthy of the Lord, to please Him in all respects, bearing fruit in every good work and increasing in the knowledge of God."

It is clear that the purpose of Paul's prayer reveals his desire for the saints to walk worthy, which is to speak of a life of holiness which pleases God. In doing so the saints would bear fruit in every good (agathos) work (ergon). The fruit produced would be beautiful and the work which would result in an increasing knowledge of the person of God.

1:11 "Strengthened with all power, according to His glorious might, for the attaining of all steadfastness and patience; joyously."

The saints would be strengthened (dunamŏō) which speaks of the enabling power of God. This is a mighty and miraculous power. He has the power and is patient with us. Also, the saints knowing that the war has already been won should help us as we patiently endure. The use of the word steadfastness (hupŏmŏnē) makes the previous point understood as it speaks of patient continuance and endurance and constancy. Joyously (chara) refers to calm delight and gladness.

1:12 "Giving thanks to the Father, who has qualified us to share in the inheritance of the saints in Light."

Once again Paul gives thanks (eucharistĕō) showing his gratefulness and gratitude to God the Father. He's grateful and thankful that God has qualified him, to enable and make able to also share (hikanŏō) in the inheritance (klērŏs), the portion, heritage, lot, of the saints of Light (phōs), which means to make manifest, to shine, to make luminous.

Paul's Prayer the Saints Would:

1. Be filled with the knowledge of His will.
2. Be filled with spiritual wisdom/understanding.
3. Walk in a manner worthy of the Lord.
4. Bear fruit in every good work.
5. Increase in real knowledge.
6. Be strengthened with all power.

Colossians 1:13-23
The Preeminent Christ

Christ is presented in this passage as the image of the invisible God. He and God are eternally related One to the other. Jesus is a reflection of God the Father, although invisible, yet real. As stated, "For it was the Father's good pleasure for all the fullness to dwell in Him" (1:19). This speaks to all the fullness of deity seen in Jesus Christ.

The Lord Jesus is also presented as preeminent, matchless, incomparable, and without an equal. Paul unveils all that God has done for us through His Son.

1:13 "For He rescued us from the domain of darkness, and transferred us to the kingdom of His beloved Son."

Christ delivered (rhuŏmai) us which is to rush or draw, i.e. to rescue or deliver from the domain (ĕxŏusia) of darkness (skŏtŏs). The domain refers to the power and authority of the dark kingdom of Satan and the evil world system. Christ exhibited His great mastery over the realm of darkness for the purpose of man's freedom. Christ then transfers (mĕthistēmi) man which means to carry away, exchange, remove, and translate to the kingdom (basilĕia) of His realm, His reign, and His royalty.

1:14 "In whom we have redemption, the forgiveness of sins."

It is in Christ that the one who has been delivered find redemption (apŏlutrōsis), or ransom in full.

Deliverance results in redemption and forgiveness (aphesis), that is freedom and pardon. The pardon of sin (hamartia), comes through the blood of Christ. Sin refers to one's offenses and missing the mark of God's holy standards, thereby not sharing in the prize.

God has done much for us through His Son, Jesus Christ.

1) God has rescued us through His Son.
2) God has removed us, transferring us to His kingdom.
3) God has redeemed us through the blood of Jesus, His Son.
4) God has brought about remission of sins through His Son.

1:15 "He is the image of the invisible God, the firstborn of all creation."

Paul states that Christ is the image (eikōn) of the invisible God. The use of the word (eikōn) means that which resembles an object, which represents it. This may also stress the fact that God is real because Jesus is real. The apostle also refers to Christ as the firstborn (prōtotokos), translated also as "first begotten." This emphasizes Christ has the relation to all creation as that of the Father. It can be stated also that Christ is above all creation. So, Paul is telling the church Jesus Christ has a prototype, God who is invisible. We may say that Christ is the image of God stamped out in the clay of humanity.

1:16 "For by Him all things were created, both in the heavens and on earth, visible and invisible, whether thrones or dominions or rulers or authorities—all things have been created through Him and for Him."

Christ is the Agent by which all things were created (ktisis), i.e. the original formation. The word comes from (ktizō) which has the idea of the proprietorship of the manufacturer, or in this case the Creator. The creation involves that in the heavens (ŏuranŏs -sky, abode of God), that which is on earth (gē ground, soil, land), dominions (kuriŏtēs – governments and rulers), rulers (archē – magistrate, principalities, rule, rank), authorities (ĕxŏusia – potentate, jurisdiction).

1:17 "He is before all things, and in Him all things hold together."

"Hold together" (sunistaō). All things hold together and are strengthened, they endure. It can be understood that in Christ all things hold together.

1:18 "He is also head of the body, the church; and He is the beginning, the firstborn from the dead, so that He Himself will come to have first place in everything."

Christ is the Head of the body (sōma), as a sound whole, the church (ĕkklēsia), the assembly of the called out, who are saints on earth or in heaven. Christ is not only the Head of the body but is also the beginning (archē) the first-born (prōtotokos) from the dead which refers to the resurrection. It is for the reason that He has first place in everything. There is a priority and a supremacy. The word "beginning" is not used to speak of Christ as being the result of God's creation but rather the cause of God's creation. Jesus could speak and create the world.

Five Attributes of Christ (Colossians 1:15-18

- He is the image of the invisible God.
- He is the first-born of all creation.
- He created all things.
- He is above all things.
- He is the Head of the body, the church.

1:19 "For it was the Father's good pleasure for all the fullness to dwell in Him."

The Father's good pleasure (ĕudŏkēō) is to think well of, to approve or to be pleased with. It is to understand that the Father was pleased that all the "fullness" (plērōma) of deity, the sum total of all divine perfection dwell (katŏikĕō), which is to reside permanently in Christ Jesus. He was fully God and fully man with a human body.

1:20 "And through Him to reconcile all things to Himself, having made peace through the blood of His cross; through Him, I say, whether things on earth or things in heaven."

Through Christ God is doing a work to bring about restoration. This is seen in the words of the apostle as the word "reconcile" (apŏkatallassō). This word speaks of setting up a relationship of peace in which restoration is made to its former condition. It deals with a relationship of peace that has been disturbed.

Romans 5:1 "Therefore, having been justified by faith, we have peace with God through our Lord Jesus Christ."

Ephesians 2:13-14 "But now in Christ Jesus you who formerly were far off have been brought near by the blood of

Christ. For He Himself is our peace, who made both groups into one and broke down the barrier of the dividing wall."
1 Peter 3:18 "For Christ also died for sins once for all, the just for the unjust, so that He might bring us to God, having been put to death in the flesh, but made alive in the spirit."

The reconciliation is made possible through the blood of His cross (staurŏs) which is seen as an instrument of His death. The term speaks of a pole, a stake, or post that is set upright. Christ has made peace through His shed blood on the cross. This peace extends to things on earth (gē) or all of the globe including heaven (ŏuranŏs), the sky, and the abode of God.

1:21 "And although you were formerly alienated and hostile in mind, engaged in evil deeds."

Paul speaks of the state of man prior to the work of reconciliation. Man was alienated (apallŏtriŏō) which is to be estranged away, to be an alien, to be a non-participant.

Romans 5:10 "For if while we were enemies we were reconciled to God through the death of His Son, much more, having been reconciled, we shall be saved by His life."

Ephesians 2:1-3, 12, "And you were dead in your trespasses and sins, in which you formerly walked according to the course of this world, according to the prince of the power of the air, of the spirit that is now working in the sons of disobedience."

Among them we too all formerly lived in the lusts of our flesh, indulging the desires of the flesh and of the mind, and were by nature children of wrath, even as the rest…remember that you were at that time separate from Christ, excluded from the commonwealth of Israel, and strangers to the covenants of promise, having no hope and without God in the world." Paul further speaks concerning the mind (dianŏis) dealing with the imagination and man's understanding. The thoughts of man were engaged in evil (pŏnērŏs) desires; things that are bad and speak of wickedness, degeneracy, maliciousness, and things that are described as vicious.

1:22 "Yet He has now reconciled you in His fleshly body through death, in order to present you before Him holy and blameless and beyond reproach—"

Once again the term reconciled (apallŏtriŏō) speaks to the work Christ accomplished on the cross. He has made possible the restoration mankind was in great need of. As stated in Colossians 1:20 Christ has made peace through the blood of His cross. As the apostle speaks about Christ's fleshly (sarx) body (sōma); this is described in 2 Corinthians 5:1-5.

"For we know that if the earthly tent which is our house is torn down, we have a building from God, a house not made with hands, eternal in the heavens. For indeed in this house we groan, longing to be clothed with our dwelling from heaven, inasmuch as we, having put it on, will not be found naked. For indeed while we are in this tent, we groan, being burdened, because we do not want to be unclothed but to be clothed, so that what is mortal will be swallowed up by life. Now He who prepared us for this very purpose is God, who gave to us the Spirit as a pledge."

So, in this life God has given to man a covering or a dwelling place referring to the fleshly body. Christ in His fleshly body through death (thanatŏs) made it possible for man

to now be presented holy and blameless (amōmŏs), which is to say one stands unblemished and faultless before holy God.
1:23 "If indeed you continue in the faith firmly established and steadfast, and not moved away from the hope of the gospel that you have heard, which was proclaimed in all creation under heaven, and of which I, Paul, was made a minister."

As the apostle speaks to those of Colossae he again reminds them of continuing in the faith (pistis), that is their conviction, credence, the religious truth they relied upon when they received Christ for salvation. The hope (ĕlpis) spoken of is one of confident expectation in the gospel (ĕuaggĕliŏn), the good news they heard proclaimed (kērussō) and published in all creation (ktisis). Paul states that he had been made a minister (diakŏnŏs) of this gospel. The apostle saw himself as a servant, an attendant, and teacher.

Colossians 1:24-29
Paul And The Hidden Mystery

Paul rejoiced in his suffering. This was to him not a personal suffering but rather it was for Christ and the benefit of the body. There was no self-pity on Paul's part. Paul was concerned with what good and benefit might come to others through his life. The apostle knew God had chosen him as a minister and entrusted him with the gospel to share. For that reason, he was a steward of the mystery of Christ and he faithfully proclaimed it to every man.

1:24 "Now I rejoice in my sufferings for your sake, and in my flesh I do my share on behalf of His body, which is the church, in filling up what is lacking in Christ's afflictions."

Paul shares with the believers that he rejoices in suffering for their sake, doing so in the flesh (sarx). The apostle was willing to do his part in representing the body (sōma) of Christ, a sound whole as the church (ĕkklēsia), a called out assembly. Christ (Christŏs) the anointed, the Messiah was Paul's motivation and his willingness to endure hardships.

1:25 "Of this church I was made a minister according to the stewardship from God bestowed on me for your benefit, so that I might fully carry out the preaching of the word of God."

The apostle was made a minister according to the stewardship (ŏikŏnŏmia) given him from God. This stewardship speaks of one who is an administrator of a household or estate. That is emphasized in the phrase, "fully carry out," (plērŏō) which is to finish a task, execute and office, and accomplish and complete what was left in one's charge. This would be done by Paul as he faithfully preached the Word of God to the benefit of the body.

1:26 "That is, the mystery which has been hidden from the past ages and generations, but has now been manifested to His saints."

The mystery is the purpose of God to gather together in one, all things in Christ. This is the great purpose God. A mystery (mustēriŏn) is a secret and is not known or been revealed. The thought is the mouth has been shut and the secret has not been spoken. The secret has been kept through the ages (aiōn) of times past. Generations (gĕnĕa), a periodof time, an age, which may speak of God's plan forthe ages. The mystery is unknown until it has been spoken or made manifest (phanĕrŏō), which is to say it has been made apparent or been declared. The mystery is clarified in Ephesians 3:5-6, "Which in other generations was not made known to the sons of men, as it has now been revealed to His holy apostles and prophets in the Spirit; to be specific, that the Gentiles are fellow heirs and fellow members of the body, and fellow partakers of the promise in Christ Jesus through the gospel." Also, the mystery is defined in Ephesians 2:14, "For He Himself is our peace, who made both groups into one and broke down the barrier of the dividing wall."

1:27 "To whom God willed to make known what is the riches of the glory of this mystery among the Gentiles, which is Christ in you, the hope of glory."

God willed to make known (gnōrizō) which is to declare, certify, and give in order that one can understand what is the riches of the glory (dŏxa), i.e, the dignity and honor among the Gentiles. The mystery is Christ in you the hope (ĕlpis), expectation and the confidence of glory.

1:28 "We proclaim Him, admonishing every man and teaching every man with all wisdom, so that we may present every man complete in Christ."

Paul proclaimed (kataggĕllō), declared, preached, and was teaching (didaskō) in order that man may learn concerning the things of Christ. He also was admonishing (nŏuthētĕō) and putting into the mind of every man with caution and all wisdom (sŏphia). Paul's purpose was to present every man complete (tēleiŏs), that is to be mature, perfect, of full age in Christ.

Ephesians 4:13 "Until we all attain to the unity of the faith, and of the knowledge of the Son of God, to a mature man, to the measure of the stature which belongs to the fullness of Christ."

1:29 "For this purpose also I labor, striving according to His power, which mightily works within me."

In order that all would come to maturity Paul was striving (agōnizŏmai) laboring actively, effectually working (energĕō) to accomplish the task of God.

Colossians 2:1-7
Built Up In Christ

2:1 "For I want you to know how great a struggle I have on your behalf and for those who are at Laodicea, and for all those who have not personally seen my face."

In the previous verses (1:28-29), the apostle stated that his purpose was to present every man mature in Christ. Here we see the heart of Paul as he speaks of the struggle (agōn) he has on their behalf. The term struggle suggests contention, great effort, and a fight. It would seem that Paul is speaking about his being involved in a contest on behalf of those who are at Colossae. This says much about Paul's heart and concern for the believers. He not only speaks to those at Colossae but for those at Laodicea as well. Paul had not been in Colossae at this point; they had not seen his face. Colossians 4:16 gives the request of the apostle to have the letter read in the church of Laodicea. This letter may have been a circular letter.

2:2 "That their hearts may be encouraged, having been knit together in love, and attaining to all the wealth that comes from the full assurance of understanding, resulting in a true knowledge of God's mystery, that is, Christ Himself,"

The desire of the apostle was to encourage the hearts of his readers. Their hearts had been knit together in love (agape), an affection, benevolence, and charity.

God is with us in strength. As their hearts are knit together it should be understood the church is our support group. Paul also desired they would attain the great wealth that comes from full assurance (plērŏphŏria) which is an entire confidence in the (epignōsis), the full knowledge of knowing the truth. The emphasis is on the mystery, which is Christ (Christŏs), the Messiah, the Anointed Col. 1:26-27).

2:3 "In whom are hidden all the treasures of wisdom and knowledge."

Paul emphasizes that all the treasures of wisdom (sŏphia) and knowledge (gnosis) are hidden in the Person of Christ. The knowledge is that of knowing and understanding. Wisdom can refer to spiritual or worldly wisdom. However, the thought is clear in the apostle's words. There is no need to search for wisdom and understanding in any other place or any other person than Christ.

Isaiah 11:2 "The Spirit of the Lord will rest on Him, The spirit of wisdom and understanding, The spirit of counsel and strength, The spirit of knowledge and the fear of the Lord."

Romans 11:33 "Oh, the depth of the riches both of the wisdom and knowledge of God! How unsearchable are His judgments and unfathomable His ways!"

James 1:5 "But if any of you lacks wisdom, let him ask of God, who gives to all generously and without reproach, and it will be given to him."

Do not look for wisdom or true knowledge in any other person or place, but Christ alone.

2:4 "I say this so that no one will delude you with persuasive argument."

The word delude (paralŏgizŏmai) speaks to enticing words, to beguile, to deceive, to seduce and mislead. This is how seduction takes place concerning false teaching. Eloquent and persuasive words can be deceiving and mislead people who are easily influenced.

Matthew 24:11 "And many false prophets will rise up and mislead many people."

Matthew 24:24 "For false Christ's and false prophets will arise and will provide great signs and wonders, so as to mislead, if possible, even the elect."

2 Peter 2:1-3 "But false prophets also appeared among the people, just as there will also be false teachers among you, who will secretly introduce destructive heresies, even denying the Master who bought them, bringing swift destruction upon themselves. Many will follow their indecent behavior, and because of them the way of the truth will be maligned; and in their greed they will exploit you with false words; their judgment from long ago is not idle, and their destruction is not asleep."

(Matthew 7:15; Mark 13:22; Colossians 2:8)

2:5 "For even though I am absent in body, I am nevertheless with you in spirit, rejoicing to see your good discipline and the stability of your faith in Christ."

In Colossians 2:1 Paul states that those at Colossae had not personally seen his face. The apostle states that he is absent (apĕmi), which means to be away. Though absent in body (sarx) he is with them in spirit (pnĕuma), the element in man by which he perceives, reflects, feels, and desires. The apostle is rejoicing concerning those at Colossae because of their good discipline (taxis) which speaks of order, and dignity. The discipline spoken of refers to that of holding a military line. Also, their stability in the faith (pistis), that is their persuasion, conviction, and truth concerning Jesus Christ.

2:6 "Therefore as you have received Christ Jesus the Lord, so walk in Him."

Paul encourages the saints to continue to live in the Lord Jesus Christ. The walk the apostle speaks of concerns their conduct, literally to say, "as you lead your life." They are to continue to walk by faith as they continue to trust and serve Christ; doing so with overflowing gratitude.

2:7 "Having been firmly rooted and now being built up in Him and established in your faith, just as you were instructed, and overflowing with gratitude."

Firmly rooted is an agricultural term. The saints are firmly rooted in Christ. Also, they are being built up (epŏikŏdŏmĕŏ) which is to rear up or build upon. It gives the picture using an architectural term. They are being built up in Christ, who is the foundation for all to build upon. The apostle speaks to the fact that the saints are being established (bebaiōō). In other words they have been taught and have a stability. So, they are following and practicing just as they had been instructed (didaskō). The saints had learned what they had been taught.

Colossians 2:8-15
Made Complete In Christ

2:8 "See to it that no one takes you captive through philosophy and empty deception, according to the tradition of men, according to the elementary principles of the world, rather than according to Christ."

Philosophy is the study of knowledge. Do not forget that Paul was dealing with the Gnostics and the error they believed. The word empty (kĕnŏs) refers to the hollowness of something that in a sense is vain an aimless. The tradition (paradŏsis) of men is that of Jewish traditionary law (precepts/ordinances) most likely. The elementary principles or the rudiments is the beginning of what we learn and would refer to as the fundamentals.

2:9 "For in Him all the fullness of Deity dwells in bodily form."

The Father was pleased that all the "fullness" (plērōma) of deity, the sum total of all divine perfection dwell (katŏikĕō), that is to reside permanently in Christ Jesus. He was fully God and fullyman with a human body.

2:10 "And in Him you have been made complete, and He is the head over all rule and authority."

He is the head because He is God. There is no rule (archē) or authority (ĕxŏusia) that stands between God and man. The term head (kĕphalē) means the sense of seizing or taking hold of. Those who are in Christ find completeness or are made full.

John 3:31 "He who comes from above is above all, he who is of the earth is from the earth and speaks of the earth. He who comes from heaven is above all."

2:11 "And in Him you were also circumcised with a circumcision made without hands, in the removal of the body of the flesh by the circumcision of Christ."

Paul states that in Christ they were circumcised (pĕritĕmnō) which means to "cut around." When one places their trust and faith in the Lord Jesus Christ God does a work in the heart of man. In a sense there is a cutting away of the body (sōma) of sins out of the flesh. The believer dies to self and is now living for Christ. The Word speaks of the new covenant written in the heart of man. In essence there is a circumcision of the heart of man.

Jeremiah 31:33 "But this is the covenant which I will make with the house of Israel after those days," declares the Lord, "I will put My law within them and on their heart I will write it; and I will be their God, and they shall be My people."

Ezekiel 36:27 "I will put My Spirit within you and cause you to walk in My statutes, and you will be careful to observe My ordinances."

2:12 "Having been buried with Him in baptism, in which you were also raised up with Him through faith in the working of God, who raised Him from the dead."

This is a deep spiritual experience that is real. We are buried within the baptism (baptisma) of His death. Thereby the individual is dead to the old life.

Romans 6:3 "Or do you not know that all of us who have been baptized into Christ Jesus have been baptized into His death?"

The apostle states the believer is raised (ĕgĕirō) and means to awaken, to rouse from death, like that of corpse through faith (pistis). This one has come to faith as the truth has been acknowledged and also accepted. Also, the use of the word dead (nĕkrŏs) refers to a corpse. In this case figuratively speaking, one who is dead in trespasses and sins (2:13).

2:13 "When you were dead in your transgressions and the un-circumcision of your flesh, He made you alive together with Him, having forgiven us all our transgressions."

The one who was dead has now been made alive (suzōŏpŏiĕō) in Him, or quickened together.

Ephesians 2:5 "Even when we were dead in our transgressions, made us alive together with Christ (by grace you have been saved)."

Paul speaks of transgressions (paraptōma) which speaks to a trespass, a fault, or an offence. When Paul speaks of un-circumcision, this designates one who is outside the promises of God.

Ephesians 2:11-12 "Therefore remember that for merly you, the Gentiles in the flesh, who are called "Un-circumcision" by the so-called "Circumcision," which is performed in the flesh by human hands— remember that you were at that time separate from Christ, excluded from the commonwealth of Israel, and strangers to the covenants of promise, having no hope and without God in the world."

However, the commitment to Christ takes place by faith and the new believer experiences forgiveness (charizŏmai), which is to be granted favor and to be forgiven freely of all transgressions.

2:14 "Having canceled out the certificate of debt consisting of decrees against us, which was hostile to us; and He has taken it out of the way, having nailed it to the cross."

The Law was the certificate of debt spoken of here. Someone has said that Satan in a sense is the one who issued a warrant for our arrest. However, Jesus took the certificate of debt and nailed it to the cross (staurŏs). The decrees (dogma) speak of the laws, the views, and ordinances. The fact that Jesus took the certificate of debt and nailed it to the cross has made forgiveness possible. Jesus is the fulfillment of the Law. He paid the price for our sin debt. We are no longer under law but now in the kingdom of grace. However, it must be understood that the cross is an affirmation of God's hatred of sin. It is also an affirmation of His steadfast determination to save humanity and the world.

2:15 "When He had disarmed the rulers and authorities, He made a public display of them, having triumphed over them through Him."

The government of Jesus' day was Rome and the religion of the day was Judaism. It was both of these that conspired to place Jesus on the cross. Jesus stripped and disarmed rulers (archē), and authorities (ĕxŏusia) and showed them for what they were.

Hebrews 2:14 "Therefore, since the children share in flesh and blood, He Himself likewise also part took of the same, that through death He might render powerless him who had the power of death, that is, the devil."

All that Jesus accomplished on the cross for fallen man is beyond human comprehension. He not only took all the sins of man for time and eternity to the cross but for all who receive Him, He has made us more than conquerors (Romans 8:37-39).

2:16 "Therefore no one is to act as your judge in regard to food or drink or in respect to a festival or a new moon or a Sabbath day—"

Paul relates to the saints at Colossae that they are not to let anyone judge (krinō) them in certain areas on the basis of the Law. The term judge speaks of letting someone pass judgment, call into question, condemn, and to distinguish concerning one's actions. Paul refused to let the Judaizers hold one to the Law. None of this was a requirement for salvation. The apostle fought the Law in regard to it being a test of salvation. There is no judge against food or drink in which there was distinguishing between that which was clean or unclean. The Sabbath day (sabbatŏn) deals with weekly observances while the festival or a new moon may speak to monthly observances. The point to be emphasized is that Paul was standing against the Judaizers and also against the legalism they were promoting.

2:17 "Things which are a mere shadow of what is to come; but the substance belongs to Christ."

The things mentioned in the previous verse are shadows or types of what is to come. Paul states that the substance (sōma) belongs to Christ. So the shadow of things to come (type) are the reality of Jesus Christ. For example, the

Day of Atonement fulfilled in Christ's death on the cross. The shadow or type teach spiritual truth. The seven feasts of the Jewish people (Israel) are rich with teaching and instruction concerning Christ. All standards one could say are fulfilled in Christ.

The Seven Feasts of Israel (Spring and Fall)

1) Passover (Pesach)
2) Unleavened Bread (Chag HaM)atzot)
3) First Fruits (Yom Habikkurim)
4) Pentecost (Shavout)
5) Trumpets (Yom Teruah)
6) Atonement (Yom Kippur)
7) Tabernacles (Sukkot)

2:18 "Let no one keep defrauding you of your prize by delighting in self-abasement and the worship of the angels, taking his stand on visions he has seen, inflated without cause by his fleshly mind."

It would appear that the Gnostics were imposing false humility (self-abasement). True humility will seldom recognize itself. The external traditions that were being practiced brought judgment to some as well as trickery and deceit. The word picture is that of a robber deceiving someone of the prize. The worship (thrēskĕia) or ceremonial observance involved angels (angĕlŏs), a messenger who was seen as a mediator to God. Visions also were involved and what was seen (hŏraō) was shared by one as an experience one perceived. This led to some being vainly puffed up by their fleshly mind (nŏus); the intellect and thought. In short, one may refer to these actions as mysticism, that teaches messages and doctrines from God can be received through visions, meditations, and dreams.

2:19 "And not holding fast to the head, from whom the entire body, being supplied and held together by the joints and ligaments, grows with a growth which is from God."

These actions took place according to Paul due to the fact that certain ones were not holding to the head (kĕphalĕ), and were away from Christ. Paul's use of the word "head" refers to that part which is most readily taken hold of. It is from Christ that the entire body is supplied and held together, thereby experiencing growth which is from God.

2:20 "If you have died with Christ to the elementary principles of the world, why, as if you were living in the world, do you submit yourself to decrees, such as…"

We are to identify with Christ in His death and His resurrection. In Christ one has died to the elementary principles (stŏichĕion) or rudiments. Therefore why would one submit to the worldly (kŏsmŏs) and its decrees. Paul states that the believers had died with Christ. If that be true, they have in Christ all that they would need.

2:21 "Do not handle, do not taste, do not touch!"

Paul exhorts the believers not to be bound to old restrictions since they had been made new in Christ. The decrees mentioned in (2:20) are defined as do not handle (haptŏmai), which means not to attach oneself or touch. Paul also mentions do not touch (thigganō), meaning to handle with the fingers. Taste (gĕuŏmai) refers to the experience of eating. All are of men (anthrōpŏs), a human being.

2:22 "(which all refer to things destined to perish with use)—in accordance with the commandments and teachings of men?"

The commandments (ĕntalma) speak of religious precepts and teachings (didaskalia) speak of the instruction and doctrine. These were doctrines of men such as holy days, circumcision, sabbath days, etc.

2:23 "These are matters which have, to be sure, the appearance of wisdom in self-made religion and self-abasement and severe treatment of the body, but are of no value against fleshly indulgence."

When the apostle speaks of the appearance of wisdom, the word appearance (lŏgŏs) refers to something thought, something said, or reasoning. The word wisdom (sŏphia) can speak of worldly or spiritual wisdom. It seems most likely that Paul is alluding to worldly wisdom as he speaks of self-made religion and self-abasement along with that of fleshly indulgence. In the context of these verses the doctrines of men sound very spiritual but are of no value. What looks like rigorous discipline is in fact a subtle form of self-indulgence. There is a lack of value in restraining sensual indulgence. Again, one who has died with Christ has all the need.

Colossians 2:16-23
Have You Been Robbed?

1) The old rituals are not needed because Christ has come.
2) Religious symbols are not needed because the Messiah has come.
3) Christ's death on the cross put an end to all the ordinances and the Law.
4) A day of rest was a commandment. This could be any day we choose top worship.
5) Let no man beguile you (rob you) of your prize. Colossians 2:18 gives the characteristics of a robber.
6) The source and matter of all true growth is found the Head (2:19).

Colossians 3:1-11
Focus, Forsake, And Follow

3:1 "Therefore if you have been raised up with Christ, keep seeking the things above, where Christ is, seated at the right hand of God."

Since (if) you have been raised with Christ and are a new creature, and are no longer dead in your transgressions there is much to share. Death was defeated and conquered in the resurrection of Christ. Paul exhorts the believers to keep seeking the things from above. The focus is no longer on the world and the things therein having been made alive with Christ. Literally it is understood that one "keeps on seeking" the things above, those things that are of God.

3:2 "Set your mind on the things above, not on the things that are on earth."

To set one's mind is to be intent on things above, it is to focus. Believers are to fall in love with the things of God, not the things of the earth (gē), the physical world and the things contained within. Seek that which is approved in heaven.

3:3 "For you have died and your life is hidden with Christ in God."

To say one has died (apŏthnēskō) is to be slain or to die off. So, the things of this earth that occupy one's time and interest are of no use. They have found life (zōē) in Christ and hidden with Christ in God. This is double security.

John 10:28-29 "And I give eternal life to them, and they will never perish; and no one will snatch them out of My hand. My Father, who has given them to Me, is greater than all; and no one is able to snatch them out of the Father's hand."

1 Peter 1:3-5 "Blessed be the God and Father of our Lord Jesus Christ, who according to His great mercy has caused us to be born again to a living hope through the resurrection of Jesus Christ from the dead, to obtain an inheritance which is imperishable and undefiled and will not fade away, reserved in heaven for you, who are protected by the power of God through faith for a salvation ready to be revealed in the last time."

2 Timothy 1:12 "For this reason I also suffer these things, but I am not ashamed; for I know whom I have believed and I am convinced that He is able to guard what I have entrusted to Him until that day."

Philippians 1:6 "For I am confident of this very thing, that He who began a good work in you will perfect it until the day of Christ Jesus."

3:4 "When Christ, who is our life, is revealed, then you also will be revealed with Him in glory."

Christ who is our life (zōē) is revealed; it will be a glorious day of great splendor and grandeur. Christ is indeed our life. Jesus said in John 11:25, "I am the resurrection and the life; he who believes in Me will live even if he dies." The apostle Paul stated in Galatians 2:20, "I have been crucified with Christ; and it is no longer I who live, but Christ lives in me; and the life which I now live in the flesh I live by faith in the Son of God, who loved me and gave Himself up for me." The use of the word revealed (phanĕrŏō) means to show, to render apparent, and to manifestly be declared. The believer will also be revealed with Christ in glory (dŏxa) when He comes again. It will be a glorious day indeed.

3:5 "Therefore consider the members of your earthly body as dead to immorality, impurity, passion, evil desire, and greed, which amounts to idolatry."

The believer is to put to death and forsake the vices and things of the old life. Prior to new life in Christ sinful habits kept one in bondage. With the new life Paul lists some actions that are sinful and no longer to be a part of the Christians life. Immorality (fornication) premarital sexual relations Impurity (akatharsia) uncleanness, impure thoughts Passion (pathŏs) inordinate affection, lust, to have unchecked passionate sexual fantasies Evil Desires (ĕpithumia) desire, lust, and longing for that which is forbidden, a sexual thirst Greed (plĕŏnĕxia) covetous practices, a desire for more

Idolatry (ĕidōlŏlatrĕia) image worship, a desire for something more than God, greed or covetousness is a gateway to idolatry.

3:6 "For it is because of these things that the wrath of God will come upon the sons of disobedience."

Wrath (ŏrgē) is a vengeance, indignation, and a justifiable punishment from God. The wrath of God is poured out simply by letting nature many times take its course. God's wrath is the consequence of man's disobedience.

3:7 "And in them you also once walked, when you were living in them."

The saints at Colossae are reminded that they also formerly had a lifestyle like that of the pagans before they had accepted Christ. When a person remembers what they were; then they will have concern forthose who are still outside the grace of God.

3:8 "But now you also, put them all aside: anger, wrath, malice, slander, and abusive speech from your mouth."

Paul now speaks of attitudes that are sinful and must be put aside. Anger (ŏrgē) violent passion, smoldering, slow burn Wrath (thumŏs) fierceness, anger out of control Malice (kakia) mean spirt, intent to do evil Slander (blasphēmia) blasphemy, evil speaking Abusive Speech – obscene language, filthy talking.

3:9 "Do not lie to one another, since you laid aside the old self with its evil practices."

Paul instructs those who have laid aside the old man to stop lying and not to be untruthful. Evil practices speaks to an act or function. In this case it is not to be the practice of the new man in Christ.

3:10 "And have put on the new self who is being renewed to a true knowledge according to the image of the One who created him—"

The new self (nĕŏs) the apostle speaks of is the man who has been regenerated and made new. This one is also being renewed (anakainŏō) or renovated to a true knowledge according to the image (ĕikōn) of One who created him, that is

Christ Jesus. This isthe purpose of God that we are to be like Jesus.

Romans 8:29 "For those whom He foreknew, He also predestined to become conformed to the image of His Son, so that He would be the firstborn among many brethren."

3:11 "A renewal in which there is no distinction between Greek and Jew, circumcised and uncircumcised, barbarian, Scythian, slave and freeman, but Christ is all, and in all."

In Christ there is no racial barrier, and no religious barrier, nor are there any social barriers. It matters not where one is from or what their background might be. Christ is all, and in all.

Colossians 3:12-17
The Christian's Wardrobe

3:12 "So, as those who have been chosen of God, holy and beloved, put on a heart of compassion, kindness, humility, gentleness and patience."

Paul previously had spoken to the believers that they were to put off certain attitudes and actions. They were to then put on the new self in which they would imitate Christ who created them. Now the apostle speaks regarding what is involved in putting on the new self. He reminds them that they have been chosen (ĕklĕktŏs) or elected by God. In that regard they are to be holy (hagiŏs) which is to be pure, blameless, and consecrated. The saints of God are beloved (agapaō) or loved much by the Father and the Son. Paul exhorts them to put on a heart (splaggehnŏn) of compassion (ŏiktirmŏs). The use of the word heart refers to an inward affection and tender mercy. Likewise, the compassion which they are to be clothed with is one of pity and mercy. The kindness (chrēstŏtēs) Paul speaks of is that of moral excellence, gentleness, and goodness. Patience is to be extended toward others. This may be defined as forbearance and is emphasized in 3:13. The child of God is to clothe himself with brotherly graces. A right relationship with God will result in a right relationship with men. This happens when one takes the time to cultivate kindness through communication with God.

3:13 "Bearing with one another, and forgiving each other, whoever has a complaint against anyone; just as the Lord forgave you, so also should you."

Bearing with (anĕchŏmai) is to endure, forbear, and to put up with. The Christian is also to forgive (charizŏmai) which is to pardon, grant as a favor, to forgive freely; this is forbearance that is put into action. Our model is that of Jesus Christ and how He so graciously has forgiven and pardoned those who now know Him as Lord and Savior. In one's previous state of lostness and being spiritually dead the Lord was gracious and patient. In 2 Peter 3:9 that truth is stated, "The Lord is not slow about His promise, as some count slowness, but is patient toward you, not wishing for any to perish but for all to come to repentance."

3:14 "Beyond all these things put on love, which is the perfect bond of unity."

Paul tells the saints that above all things they are to put on love (agapē). This love is best described as charity, affection, and benevolence. It is called the perfect bond. It may be said that love is the belt that holds all the virtues that one puts on in this spiritual wardrobe. This love brings about unity (tĕlĕlŏtēs), that which is completeness and also perfection.

3:15 "Let the peace of Christ rule in your hearts, to which indeed you were called in one body; and be thankful."

The peace (ĕirĕnē) spoken of deals with a quietness and a rest. To let the peace of Christ rule in the heart is to sense a peace from God. To sense turmoil in one's spirit is to know that Christ who is in you reveals something is amiss. The heart (kardia) of man deals with the thoughts, feelings, mind, will, and emotions. Being a finite being and knowing Christ is to allow Him to call the balls and strikes in one's life. Let His peace act as the arbiter in all decision making. Thankful (ĕucharistŏs) Christians are to be grateful people knowing they are favored. Believers are called to live as one united body (sōma) and always being thankful.

3:16 "Let the word of Christ richly dwell within you, with all wisdom teaching and admonishing one another with psalms and hymns and spiritual songs, singing with thankfulness in your hearts to God."

The words (lŏgŏs) of Christ and all He spoke and said in His discourses should abide in those who are believers. The richness of the teachings of Christ should find a special place in the hearts of every child of God. Teaching (didaskō) and imparting truth is a two-way street as the saints admonish (nŏuthĕtĕō) or caution one another putting into the mind the words of Christ. This admonishing also takes place with all spiritual wisdom (sŏphia) with psalms (psalmŏs), hymns (humnŏs), and spiritual (pnĕumatkŏs) songs (ōdē) that teach the Word of God. Singing should be dedicated to the Lord with thankfulness (charis) and joy in the heart (kardia).

3:17 "Whatever you do in word or deed, do all in the name of the Lord Jesus, giving thanks through Him to God the Father."

Whatever is done in word (lŏgŏs) or in deed (ĕrgŏn) is to be done in the name of the Lord Jesus. To do something in His name (ŏnŏma) is to do for One who is of authority. One's speech, work, and actions are to be done as if it were being done for God. These actions are to be done with thankfulness (ĕucharistĕō) and with gratefulness and gratitude.

Precepts of Life
Colossians 3:17-25

1. Life without love isn't much. (3:14)
    A. Love is true self-hood.
    B. Love grows and develops.
    C. Love is something humans cannot live without.
    D. Love is a vital part of your relationship with others.
    E. Love is unselfish. (1 Corinthians 13)

2. You have to belong. (3:15)
    You are created to have fellowship with God.

3. Don't stop learning. (3:16)
    A. Learning will improve your personality.
    B. Colossians 2:3 – Jesus is truth.

4. Make your unique contribution. (3:17)
    A. What will your greatest contribution be?
    B. Are you making your maximum contribution to the world and God?
    C. Basic Desire – to make a contribution.
    D. Most Important Desire – lead someone to Christ.

5. You cannot live with guilt. (3:24-25)
    A. Guilt will destroy you.
    B. Guilt and sin are too big for men to live with.
    C. Confession is the key.

Colossians 3:18-4:1
Family And Work Relationships

God has a divine order and design regarding family and other relationships. The relationships that appear in this section of Scripture (3:18-4:1) are assigned roles as well as responsibilities. The different relationships spoken of are that of the husband and wife, the slave and the master, and one must not forget the relationship that the believer has with the Lord. The relationship the believer has with the Lord is of great importance and will determine how each behaves and responds to one another.

God assigns a role and a responsibility to the wife and also to the husband. As the apostle speaks concerning the family relationships the roles and responsibilities of each are defined according to the will of God and revealed in the Scriptures. Genesis 2:18-24 is where we find God's first words about the family. "Then the Lord God said, "It is not good for the man to be alone; I will make him a helper suitable for him." Out of the ground the Lord God formed every beast of the field and every bird of the sky, and brought them to the man to see what he would call them; and whatever the man called a living creature, that was its name. The man gave names to all the cattle, and to the birds of the sky, and to every beast of the field, but for Adam there was not found a helper suitable for him. So, the Lord God caused a deep sleep to fall upon the man, and he slept; then He took one of his ribs and closed up the flesh at that place. The Lord God fashioned into a woman the rib which He had taken from the man, and brought her to the man. The man said, "This is now bone of my bones, And flesh of my flesh; She shall be called Woman, Because she was taken out of Man." For this reason a man shall leave his father and his mother, and be joined to his wife; and they shall become one flesh."

The role of the wife is seen as that of the helper and her responsibility is one of submitting to the husband. His role is seen as one of leadership while his responsibility is to love his wife as Christ loved the church. Today's culture and society finds itself in total disagreement with the Word of God and His design for the family as He has ordained it to be. The Scriptures will be the authority for the relationships discussed in this section of Scripture.

3:18 "Wives, be subject to your husbands, as is fitting in the Lord."

The wife is to be subject (hupŏtasō) meaning to be subordinate, to obey, to be under, and to submit to the leadership of the husband. Submission means the wife place herself or she organizes herself under her husband according to God's command. Literally she is submitting herself first to the Lord.

1 Corinthians 11:3 "But I want you to understand that Christ is the head of every man, and the man is the head of a woman, and God is the head of Christ."

Ephesians 5:23 "For the husband is the head of the wife, as Christ also is the head of the church, He Himself being the Savior of the body."

1 Peter 3:1 "In the same way, you wives, be submissive to your own husbands so that even if any of them are disobedient to the word, they may be won without a word by the behavior of their wives"

3:19 "Husbands, love your wives and do not be embittered against them."

The husband has been given the role of leader by God. With that role comes the responsibility to love (agapaō) which is a sacrificial love, a purifying love, a protective love, a caring love, and a love that is unbreakable. Again, God's Word is the guide and the blueprint given for the family.

Ephesians 5:22-23 "Wives, be subject to your own husbands, as to the Lord. For the husband is the head of the wife, as Christ also is the head of the church, He Himself being the Savior of the body. But as the church is subject to Christ, so also the wives ought to be to their husbands in everything. Husbands, love your wives, just as Christ also loved the church and gave Himself up for her, so that He might sanctify her, having cleansed her by the washing of water with the word, that He might present to Himself the church in all her glory, having no spot or wrinkle or any such thing; but that she would be holy and blameless. So, husbands ought also to love their own wives as their own bodies. He who loves his own wife loves himself; for no one ever hated his own flesh, but nourishes and cherishes it, just as Christ also does the church, because we are members of His body. For this reason a man shall leave his father and mother and shall be joined to his wife, and the two shall become one flesh. This mystery is great; but I am speaking with reference to Christ and the church. Nevertheless, each individual among you also is to love his own wife even as himself, and the wife must see to it that she respects her husband."

3:20 "Children, be obedient to your parents in all things, for this is well-pleasing to the Lord."

The apostle turns now to the children of the family. Children are to be obedient (hupakŏuō) which has very similar meaning to that of submission spoken of previously regarding the wife. The term speaks of someone who is subordinate to hear and to listen attentively. As children obey this is well-pleasing (ĕuarĕstŏs) to the Lord (kuriŏs) or fully agreeable.

Exodus 20:12 ""Honor your father and your mother, that your days may be prolonged in the land which the Lord your God gives you."

Ephesians 6:1-3 "Children, obey your parents in the Lord, for this is right. Honor your father and mother (which is the first commandment with a promise), so that it may be well with you, and that you may live long on the earth."

3:21 "Fathers, do not exasperate your children, so that they will not lose heart."

God instructs parents not to exasperate (ĕrĕthizō) which is to provoke to anger which may come from the parent who tries to over correct. J.B. Phillips translates it, "Fathers, don't over-correct your children, or you will take all the heart out of them."

3:22 "Slaves, in all things obey those who are your masters on earth, not with external service, as those who merely please men, but with sincerity of heart, fearing the Lord."

In this section (3:22-4:1) Paul speaks of the master and slave relationships. While this may not be a relationship seen in society today, the application is one that can be viewed in the employer-employee relationship. However, in either regard it is clear that the bitterness is taken out of the institution of both relationships.

The term slaves (dŏulŏs) speaks of one that is under subjection or subserviency. As the master speaks to the slave he is to obey (hupakŏuō), that is to listen attentively and to conform to the command of that one who is superior in authority. Master (kuriŏs) is a term in which one would refer to them as lord, sir, controller, and master. When Paul speaks of the servant obeying, he stresses that it is not to be with external service (ŏphthalmŏdŏulĕia). This is to mean eye service. It also suggests that this is a person who might need watching due to the fact that they only work when the master or the employer is watching. When this is done, they are only doing it to be pleasing to men (anthrōparsĕkŏ) or to be a man pleaser, courting the attention of man. When the slave obeys it is to be with sincerity (haplŏtēs) which is without self-seeking or without dissimulation, fearing (phŏbĕō) the Lord; this is respect and reverence.

3:23 "Whatever you do, do your work heartily, as for the Lord rather than for men."

The apostle uses here the word heartily as in his speaking of the work being done. Heartily comes come from two words (ĕk) which means out from and (psuchē) which refers to the soul. Literally the obedience to the task given comes from the soul.

In the heart of the servant he is doing this for the Lord rather than man (anthrōpos), a human being. J.B. Phillips translates the verse in this manner, whatever your task is, put your whole heart and soul into it, as into work done for the

Lord and not merely for men, knowing that your real reward will come from Him."

3:24 "Knowing that from the Lord you will receive the reward of the inheritance. It is the Lord Christ whom you serve."

The servant is first of all a servant of the Lord. In keeping that in mind he is aware that his reward as stated previously comes from the Lord. Paul uses the word receive (apŏlambanō), which means to receive in full. Again, it should be noted that the term serve (dŏuleuō) speaks to the fact that this person is a slave and in bondage to his Master, the Lord (kuriŏs). It should be emphasized that servants serve while slaves are owned. The saint has been bought with a price and is not his own. The servant is to keep in mind that his reward of the inheritance (klērŏnŏmia), his heirship, and possession will come from the Lord.

3:25 "For he who does wrong will receive the consequences of the wrong which he has done, and that without partiality."

This verse could be summed up this way, "You get what you deserve." Choices are made by many but no one can choose the consequences. The one who does wrong will receive judgment and it will be without partiality (prŏsōpŏlēpsia), without any favoritism or respect of person.

4:1 "Masters, grant to your slaves justice and fairness, knowing that you too have a Master in heaven."

Masters are to a treat their servants as they would have their heavenly Master treat them. Paul speaks here of justice (dikaiŏs), that which is just, holy, and righteous. Also, he speaks of fairness (isŏtēs) to speak of likeness and equity. As one remembers that he too has a Master in heaven (ŏuranŏs) his actions should lead him to treat his slaves or employees as he himself desires to be treated by the Lord.

Colossians 4:2-6
Devoted Prayer And Godly Conduct

In this final chapter Paul encourages and exhorts the believers to be devoted in prayer and as they walk about to be mindful of how they walk.

4:2 "Devote yourselves to prayer, keeping alert in it with an attitude of thanksgiving."

Paul exhorts the believers to devote (prŏskartĕrĕō) themselves to prayer. To devote is to be diligent, to be constantly praying, to be continually praying, and to be persistent. The apostle references the subject of prayer (prŏsĕuchē) which can be described as earnestly praying. The idea is to "keep on" praying as Jesus stated in the Sermon on the Mount. The context is to keep on asking, keep on seeking, and to keep on knocking.

Matthew 7:7 ""Ask, and it will be given to you; seek, and you will find; knock, and it will be opened to you."

4:3 "Praying at the same time for us as well, that God will open up to us a door for the word, so that we may speak forth the mystery of Christ, for which I have also been imprisoned."

Praying (prŏsĕuchŏmai) is to pray to God which involves supplication or to make requests of God. One may see that Paul is asking them to be specific in their praying. As they are devoted to prayer the apostle is asking them at the same time (hama) they are together to pray that God will open a door for the opportunity of the word (lŏgŏs) to go forth in divine expression and utterance. Specifically, Paul speaks of the mystery (mustĕriŏn) of Christ for which he has been imprisoned. The mystery refers to the Gospel message that has been revealed to the Gentiles as the apostle had preached to them. Colossians 1:25-27 defines this mystery as spoken by Paul, "Of this church I was made a minister according to the stewardship from God bestowed on me for your benefit, so that I might fully carry out the preaching of the word of God, that is, the mystery which has been hidden from the past ages and generations, but has now been manifested to His saints, to whom God willed to make known what is the riches of the glory of this mystery among the Gentiles, which is Christ in you, the hope of glory." Paul's request is specific as what is to be prayed for. Often many prayers are offered in generalities rather than with specificity.

4:4 "That I may make it clear in the way I ought to speak."

The apostle's desire was that he might make it clear (phanĕrŏō) which means to render apparent. Paul desired to make the most of the opportunity that God would provide for him to preach the Gospel. In doing so to declare the Gospel and make it manifest was his primary motive, knowing that the Word of God would not return void and lives would forever be changed.

4:5 "Conduct yourselves with wisdom toward outsiders, making the most of the opportunity."

Conduct yourselves (pĕripatĕō) carries the meaning that as one treads all around, walks about, and lives, they are to do so with spiritual wisdom and to walk rightly. Believers are to make the most (ĕxagŏrazō) of the opportunities presented to them. That is, they are to buy up the time, redeem the time, and rescue it from being lost. As believers are walking about with wisdom they must be wise, to redeem the time, and they must be aware of the outsiders (ĕxō) they encounter. These are those who are away from God and have no knowledge of Christ as He stated in Mark 4:11, "And He was saying to them, "To you has been given the mystery of the kingdom of God, but those who are outside get everything given in parables."

4:6 "Let your speech always be with grace, as though seasoned with salt, so that you will know how you should respond to each person."

Paul instructs believers to let their speech (lŏgŏs) always be with grace (charis). Their speech and communication as they share Christ is to be one of divine influence upon the heart of the lost with graciousness, being acceptable with favor. The speech is to be seasoned with salt. Salt is used for purification, preservation, and taste. Perhaps one may think of creating a thirst in one's life as they hear the message of the Gospel of grace go forth.

Devoted Prayer Is:
- Persistent Prayer (4:2a)
- Watchful Prayer (4:2b)
- Thankful Prayer (4:2c)
- Specific Prayer (4:3)
- Committed Prayer (4:4)

Colossians 4:7-18
Paul's Co-Laborers In The Ministry

4:7-8 "As to all my affairs, Tychicus, our beloved brother and faithful servant and fellow bond-servant in the Lord, will bring you information. For I have sent him to you for this very purpose, that you may know about our circumstances and that he may encourage your hearts."

Five times in the New Testament we find the name of Tychicus mentioned. Tychicus had accompanied Paul previously when possibly carrying the collection to Jerusalem. He may have been a delegate of his church (Acts 20:4). It appears that Paul saw him as his representative to the church at Colossae. He was a man that was well trusted according to Paul's words as he refers to him as a faithful servant and also, as a fellow bond-servant. He was also seen as an encourager. As Paul's co-laborer, Tychicus would inform them regarding all of his affairs and circumstances. Tychicus had also accompanied the apostle in his journeys as a missionary and had carried the letter of Ephesians.

4:9 "And with him Onesimus, our faithful and beloved brother, who is one of your number. They will inform you about the whole situation here."

Onesimus was a runaway slave from a man named Philemon. Paul had won him to the Lord while he was a runaway. He is described as faithful and beloved. He helped deliver the Colossians Epistle.

Onesimus has been called by some a man with a bad background. It is interesting his name means *useful*.

It would seem that he had stolen from his master and had fled. The providence of God can be seen in the circumstances as Onesimus came to the saving knowledge of Christ. Some conclude that as a runaway slave he was not living up to his name. Once he came to know Christ he now was useful to Paul and could be to his master. Thus, he could now live up to his name.

4:10 "Aristarchus, my fellow prisoner, sends you his greetings; and also Barnabas's cousin Mark (about whom you received instructions; if he comes to you, welcome him)."

Aristarchus by many is referred to a burden bearer. This is emphasized by Spiros Zodhiates in his notes and commentary concerning Aristarchus. He states, "The first reference to Aristarchus in Acts 19:29 describes him as Paul's fellow traveler when seized by the Ephesian mob. In Acts 20:4 he accompanies Paul to Jerusalem, probably as an official Thessalonian delegate with the collection, and in Acts 27:2 he is in a ship with Paul as they sail to Caesarea. He possibly joined Paul and became a fellow prisoner, possibly alternating with Epaphras in voluntary imprisonment (Philemon 23, 24)."

Mark is spoken of at times as a man with a second chance. In Acts 15:36-40 a dispute takes place in regards to Mark between Paul and Barnabas. At the time of the first missionary journey Mark had left and returned home. There has been over the years much speculation as to why Mark returned home. It has been stated that he had gotten homesick. It will continue to be a topic of much speculation as to exactly what took place. However, the end of the matter for most is revealed by Paul in his final words. In 2 Timothy 4:11 the aged apostle says "Bring Mark, for he is useful to me in service." It would appear that whatever the division was with Paul, Barnabas, and Mark it was a settled issue. The fact that Barnabas was an encourager through the Scriptures most likely had a great role to play in the resolution of the problem. When one thinks of John Mark two questions should be answered. Have you written anybody off? Do you have a John Mark in your life?

4:11 "And also Jesus who is called Justus; these are the only fellow workers for the kingdom of God who are from the circumcision, and they have proved to be an encouragement to me."

Perhaps this statement brings back a few memories, "All the world is a stage but nobody wants to be a stagehand." Justus represents all those who serve but are never in the spotlight. This is one who will do the little tasks that need to be done. When one thinks of Justus they can think of a team player. A great need exists for such as these. Everyone needs a Justus in their life, one with a servant's heart and one with a servant's spirit.

4:12-13 "Epaphras, who is one of your number, a bond slave of Jesus Christ, sends you his greetings, always laboring earnestly for you in his prayers, that you may stand perfect and fully assured in all the will of God. For I testify for him that he has a deep concern for you and for those who are in Laodicea and Hierapolis."

Epaphras was most likely the founder of the church of Colossae. Many things characterize this man. He is described as a bond slave of the Lord Jesus Christ, one who labors earnestly in prayer, and one who has a deep concern for the saints at Colossae, Laodicea, and Hierapolis. In Colossians 1:7 Paul referred to him as a faithful servant (sundŏulōs), which is to say he is a co-slave. Looking at Epaphras and the dedication he exhibited causes one to stop and reflect on their own life as a child of God. How would someone describe you as a fellow servant and co-laborer?

4:14 "Luke, the beloved physician, sends you his greetings, and also Demas."

In this passage we have a stark contrast between two individuals. Luke was a gifted man. According to the volume Luke wrote more of the New Testament than all the others. He was the only Gentile writer. Luke stayed with Paul to the very end of Paul's life. However, Demas was a man who gave up. Paul states in 2 Timothy 4:10 "For Demas, having loved this present world, has deserted me and gone to Thessalonica; Crescens has gone to Galatia, Titus to Dalmatia." Demas is the only one of Paul's companions about whom he says nothing. Luke the beloved physician stayed close to Paul to the end as a friend that stays close to a brother. Demas who loved the world forsook Paul perhaps for the pleasures that beckoned him back to the things of the world.

4:16-18 "When this letter is read among you, have it also read in the church of the Laodiceans; and you, for your part read my letter that is coming from Laodicea. Say to Archippus, "Take heed to the ministry which you have received in the Lord, that you may fulfill it." I, Paul, write this greeting with my own hand. Remember my imprisonment. Grace be with you."

Some scholars suggest that Paul's letter from Laodicea may have been lost. Others believe that this letter was actually the letter to the Ephesians. The fact is that none are sure as to what happened to the letter or if it truly was the Ephesian letter. Paul exhorts Archippus to fulfill the ministry he had received. The church met in the home of Archippus as we find in Philemon 2. Finally, Paul closes the letter in his own hand with the final greeting of grace and peace. In his closing he asks for prayer regarding his imprisonment. Though the messenger was imprisoned the Word would continue to go forth unhindered.

Philemon

Paul addressed this letter to Philemon. The question has been asked as to why this letter was preserved and a part of Scripture. N.T. Wright states, "It is unlikely that the letter would have been preserved if it had not been received in the spirit in which it was sent. We are on safe ground in postulating a happy ending to the story. The reconciliation of Philemon and Onesimus becomes an acted parable of the gospel itself, which breaks into the world of sin, suspicion and anger, of pride and fear, and the good news that Jesus Christ has revealed God's purposes of salvation, of human wholeness, of loving and forgiving fellowship."

Paul opens the letter and refers to himself as a prisoner of Jesus Christ. This is the only place in his salutations that he refers to himself in that way. However, Rome would see Paul as a prisoner of Rome. Timothy is Paul's fellow worker since his second missionary journey. Timothy was a great aid in Paul's ministry and the apostle always gave recognition to those who aided him in his ministry.

Verses 2-7 emphasizes his appreciation and prayers for the church in the home of Archippus. The church was most likely at Colossae, a single house church. Paul's wish for them is grace and peace that comes from God the Father and the Lord Jesus Christ. Paul was a man always praying and taking on the burden of the entire church. This included places where he had been as well as places where he had not been. Paul may have done more in his prayer life in prison than while out evangelizing. Paul is reporting to them how he has heard of their love and faith for all the saints and also for the Lord Jesus Christ. Some refer to verse 6 as the main verse as Paul speaks concerning fellowship (kŏinŏnia). This is described as communication, partnership, and fellowship. Paul reveals his heart in verse 7 as he shares the joy and comfort that has refreshed his heart because of Philemon.

After Paul's greeting and words of appreciation he begins to make his appeals. The apostle is trying to get Philemon and Onesimus together. He had won them both to the Lord. Paul states to Philemon that he has enough confidence to order him to do that which is right. However, Paul appeals for love's sake to do that which is proper. Also, Paul refers to himself as the aged pastor which may lead Philemon to have some thought of pity. It seems that there would be no doubt that Philemon would do as Paul had asked since he too had been won to the Lord by the apostle (verse 19). In his appeal Paul speaks of the slave Onesimus as his child whom he had begotten in his imprisonment. It is interesting that Paul uses a play on words regarding the name of Onesimus. His name means "useful." Paul in his appeal states that Onesimus formerly was "useless" to Philemon but now he is "useful" to them both (verses 10-11).

Paul had to send Onesimus back that was the right thing to do morally. Paul makes it clear that Onesimus is very dear to him as if he is sending his very heart. He had the desire to keep Onesimus as he would aid and be of a great benefit to Paul in his imprisonment. Again, Paul's words would tug at the heart of Philemon as he appeals to him that he desired the decision to be one of his own free will (verses 12-14).

Paul speaks concerning the providence of God. He states that perhaps Onesimus was separated from Philemon for a time in order that he might have him back forever. Onesimus would now be a fellow brother and not seen as a slave.

Whatever Onesimus' debt was to his master, Paul was willing to pay. He told Philemon to charge it to his account. This is a great reminder to all who know Christ as their Savior and Lord. For it was Christ who took all of our debt (sin) upon Himself when He was crucified on the cross. Paul reminds Philemon that he too is indebted. The apostle reminds Philemon that he owed his own self to Paul. He presses Philemon to refresh his heart and let him benefit from him in the Lord (verses 15-20).

In Paul's closing remarks he reveals his confidence in Philemon knowing that he will do "even more" than what he had asked. Love indeed will go the second mile.

Philemon

Theme: Christian Courtesy, Christian Brotherhood, Forgiveness, The Law of Love, The Saving Power of Jesus Christ.

Characters: Paul, Philemon, Onesimus

Colossians 4:9 - Paul calls Onesimus, "Our faithful and beloved brother, who is one of your number." Paul is speaking of Philemon's slave who had ran away.

Throughout the Epistle the appeal is based on the reality of the love of Christ which makes all Christians one family. Faith in Christ is the source from which all love comes.

1. The Apostle's Appreciation (1-7)
    A. Paul expresses his deep love.
    B. Paul emphasizes the brotherhood of all Christians. (1-2)
    C. Paul's Ministry: Team Operation
    D. Fellowship (6)
    a. We belong to one another.
    b. We are mutually identified.
    c. There is mutual participation.

2. The Apostle's Plea (8-16)
    A. Paul has a request which is to get Philemon and Onesimus together.
    B. Paul makes five appeals.
    a. (8) Philemon's testimony and reputation.
    b. (9) Christian love
    c. (10) The conversion of Onesimus

d. (11-14) The usefulness of Onesimus
e. (15-16) The providence of God.
Onesimus' Salvation Philemon and Onesimus are brother for eternity.

3. The Apostle's Promise (17-25)
    A. Partner (koinonia – fellowship)
    B. (17) Receive – receive into one's family.
    C. (18) Charge that to my account.
    a. The Cross
    b. "It is finished."
    D. (19) Philemon is indebted.
    E. (20) "Refresh my spirit."
    F. (21) "Do even more" – love will go the second mile.

Application:

1. No Christian has the right to refuse one who God has welcomed.
2. Justification by faith results in fellowship by faith.
3. The one thing above all that people need is to be received.

The Cross: He paid our debt, took our punishment, gave us righteousness if we (you) trust in Him.

Works Cited

Alpha-Omega Ministries Inc. *The Preacher's Sermon & Outline Bible,* Galatians, Ephesians, Philippians, and Colossians, Christian Publishers & Ministries, King, NC, ©1991.

Dr. Jerry Breazeale, an Exegesis on Colossians, New Orleans Baptist Theological Seminary Classroom Lectures. Classroom Notes. © 1988.

Tommy C. Higle, *Becoming All God Wants You To Be,* A Study In Colossians. Tommy Higle Publishers, Inc., Marietta, OK, © 2010.

John MacArthur, Jr. *The MacArthur New Testament Commentary*, Colossians & Philemon. Moody Press, Chicago, Ill, © 1992.

J. Vernon McGee, *Thru The Bible*, 1 Corinthians thru Revelation, Volume 5. Thomas Nelson Publishers, Nashville, TN, © 1983.

J.B. Phillps, *The New Testament in Modern English*, Galahad Books, New York, NY, © 1972.

Warren w. Wiersbe, *The Bible Exposition Commentary,* Volume 2, Ephesians – Revelation. Victor Books, Wheaton, Ill, © 1989.

Harold L. Willmington, *The Outline Bible*, Tyndale Publishers, Inc. Wheaton, Ill, © 1999.

Dr. Bruce Wilkinson, *A Biblical Portrait of Marriage*, Walk Thru The Bible Publications, Atlanta, GA, © *2001*.

N.T. Wright, *Colossians and Philemon*, Tyndale New Testament Commentaries, Inter-Varsity Press, Leicester, England. William B. Eerdmans Publishing Company, Grand Rapids, MI, © 1986.

Spiros Zodhiates, ThD., *The Hebrew-Greek Study Bible*, NASB. Chattanooga, TN. AMG Publishers, © *1990*.

G.O.S.P.E.L.
(The Good News)

G – God <u>loves</u> you.

John 3:16 "For <u>God so loved</u> the world, that He gave His only begotten Son, that whoever believes in Him shall not perish, but have eternal life."

O – God <u>offered</u> His Son.

Romans 5:8 "But God demonstrates His own love toward us, in that while we were yet sinners, <u>Christ died for us</u>."

1 Corinthians 15:1, 3-4 "Now I make known to you, brethren, the gospel which I preached to you, which also you received, in which also you stand, For I delivered to you as of first importance what I also received, that <u>Christ died for our sins</u> according to the Scriptures, and that He was buried, and that <u>He was raised on the third day</u> according to the Scriptures."

S – <u>Sin</u> is a fact.

Romans 3:23 "For all have <u>sinned</u> and fall short of the glory of God."

P – There is, a <u>penalty</u> for sin, someone has to pay that penalty.

Romans 6:23 "For the wages of sin is <u>death</u>, but the gift of God is eternal life in Christ Jesus our Lord."

Hebrews 9:27 "And inasmuch as it is appointed for men to die once and after this comes the judgment."

E – God extends the invitation to receive His Son as Savior.

2 Peter 3:9 "The Lord is not slow about His promise as some count slowness, but is patient toward you, not wishing for any to perish but for all to come to repentance."

Revelation 3:20 "Behold I stand at the door and knock; if anyone hears my voice and opens the door, I will come in to him and will dine with him, and he with Me."

L – Life can be your today.

1 John 5:11-12 "And the testimony is this, that God has given us eternal life, and this life is in His Son. He who has the Son has the life; he who does not have the Son of God does not have the life."

All Scripture quotations are taken from the New American Standard Bible, © 1995, by the Lockman Foundation.

About The Author

Dr. Billy J. Owensby is a native of Commerce, Georgia. He is married to Deborah (Poole) Owensby. They have two grown children, Jeremy and Ryan who are both married. Dr. Owensby and his wife Deborah have six grandchildren and four great grandchildren.

Currently Dr. Owensby is serving as the Discipleship Pastor of Nails Creek Baptist Church in Homer, Georgia. He has also pastored other church in Louisiana and in Northeast Georgia. He is the founder of North Georgia Baptist Theological Seminary (www.ngbts.com).

Dr. Owensby has authored other works in addition to this study on Colossians.

- The Expositor's Notes: Selected Sermons
- The Expositor's Notes: 1 Timothy
- The Expositor's Notes: 1-2-3 John (Genuine Christianity)
- Ephesians: Breaking Down The Walls
- James: From Belief To Behavior
- Revelation, The Time Is Near
- Jonah, The Runaway Prophet
- The Shepherd Psalm (Psalm 23)
- The Prophetic Story of the Kinsman Redeemer (Studies In Ruth)

Any of the following studies can be acquired by sending a request to the email: drbjowensby@gmail.com.

www.ingramcontent.com/pod-product-compliance
Lightning Source LLC
LaVergne TN
LVHW041540060526
838200LV00037B/1075